The Key to
The Da Vinci Code

Stewart Ferris

Crombie Jardine
PUBLISHING LIMITED
13 Nonsuch Walk, Cheam, Surrey, SM2 7LG
www.crombiejardine.com

This edition was first published by
Crombie Jardine Publishing Limited in 2005

ISBN 1-905102-22-4

Written by Stewart Ferris
Cover design by Alastair Williams

Cover images:
Vitruvian Man by Leonardo da Vinci
and *Les Bergers d'Arcadie* by Nicolas Poussin

Printed and bound in the United Kingdom by
William Clowes Ltd, Beccles, Suffolk

**Note: This book has not been approved or endorsed
by Dan Brown or any individual or entity connected
to *The Da Vinci Code*.**

About the author

Stewart Ferris first visited Rennes-le-Château in 1983 and has recently written and presented a documentary in which he investigates theories about the source of the sudden wealth of its nineteenth-century village priest, Bérenger Saunière. It is some of these theories upon which Dan Brown based the theme of *The Da Vinci Code*. Stewart is also the author of more than twenty other books, published in seven languages.

For photographs to accompany this book visit www.stewartferris.com.

for Katia

Contents

The key to
The Da Vinci Code's
success

Dan Brown's novel *The Da Vinci Code* has been a phenomenal bestseller, with millions of copies of the book sold in 42 languages. It's a pacy, well-structured thriller with plenty of twists and turns; a classic page-turner that's hard to put down. A snippet of information or a clue appears in every chapter, a kind of cliffhanger that is not immediately explained. But the following chapter doesn't always resolve it: Dan Brown switches between plot and subplot, each story strand containing its own cliffhangers, and each storyline wrapped around the other so that by the time the reader has found the answer to one tantalising clue, another one has appeared. The engrossed follower has no option but to continue with the story at break-neck speed. But is that enough to explain the novel's popularity?

The answer lies in the concepts dealt with in *The Da Vinci Code*. The book is a complex blend of symbolism, historical theories, secret societies and religion, which separately presented would make for some heavy reading. When the information is filtered through to the reader in the context of a novel, however, a much wider audience is exposed to the ideas in the book than would otherwise be possible. Dan Brown has created a modern day Grail quest, and in doing so has revitalised, and to some extent reinvented, an ancient literary tradition that extends back to the famous fourteenth-century poem *Sir Gawain and the Green Knight* and to earlier written and oral poems.

Admittedly, Grail quests have always been popular, but never *this* popular. What has Dan Brown done that is so different?

How can the hunt for the Grail be so fascinating to people living in the Internet Age?

The answer is fundamental to the novel, to history and to Christian religion, for it concerns the meaning of the word 'Grail'. Medieval Grail manuscripts used the word 'Sangraal', which was later split into 'San Graal', meaning Holy Grail. But the authors of one of the books that influenced Dan Brown, *The Holy Blood and the Holy Grail*, suggested that perhaps the word had been split in the wrong place. If instead of 'San Graal' the split is changed to make 'Sang Raal' then the meaning changes to 'Royal Blood'.

Therefore the quest for the Holy Grail changes from a relatively meaningless hunt for a chalice artefact to a search for a holy bloodline – the bloodline of Jesus.

Since the gospels that were chosen for inclusion in the Bible by the Roman Emperor Constantine in the fourth century were only those that dealt with Jesus as a divine figure (any writings about Jesus as a man were discarded and suppressed) the Bible contains no references to the personal life of Jesus.

If it were the case that Jesus had been married and had fathered one or more children, this may have created a need in subsequent centuries for the Church to find and destroy any surviving descendants so that the truth of the official gospels could not be cast in doubt.

Hence the search for the Holy Grail has a new meaning – one that makes new sense of historical facts.

If you read *The Da Vinci Code* and choose to accept the message behind it, suddenly the last two thousand years of European history take on a different perspective. That is the true reason for the novel's success.

The absence of any writings in the Bible about the first thirty years of Jesus' life, the ferocity with which heretical branches of Christianity were eradicated in the Middle Ages, the discovery in 1945 of the hidden Nag Hammadi manuscripts containing gospels that were banished by the early Church: all these things and more seem to slot more neatly into the jigsaw of history than they did before.

Whether the reader believes the theories in *The Da Vinci Code* or not, the book at least raises questions about Christianity and what it stands for. Not everyone agrees with Dan Brown, and not all of the 'facts' as presented in the novel are correct, but at least people are now discussing ideas about a branch of religion that may have been taken for granted for too long.

The story
in a nutshell

The plot of *The Da Vinci Code* begins as a murder mystery but quickly develops into a chase in which the protagonists, Robert Langdon and Sophie Neveu, must find the Holy Grail before the bad guys, Sir Leigh Teabing and Silas.

If they don't get there first then the truth about the Grail could be lost forever.

After the reader has been led through a labyrinth of clues, the nature of the Grail is revealed to be the bloodline of Jesus, and a huge amount of background information is included in the dialogue and narrative in order to justify that theory.

The ironic twist in the story is that Sophie searches for the Grail only to discover that it is within her, that she herself is a direct descendant of Jesus and that many people have died in order to protect her from religious extremists.

The key to the major characters in the novel and the symbolism in their names

Jacques Saunière

The name of the character who dies in the Louvre at the beginning of the novel is Dan Brown's way of linking his story to the mystery of Rennes-le-Château and the priest of that village, Bérenger Saunière.

Saunière's name is the fourth word to appear in the novel, thus the major theme of the plot is hinted at immediately.

The fictional Saunière is the Grand Master of the Priory of Sion, a secret organisation said in the novel to have acted as protector of the Holy Grail for a thousand years. In reality the Priory probably died out in medieval times, if it ever existed.

Both real and fictional Saunières were obsessive about creating riddles and clues. The real one left dozens of them in and around the church that he rebuilt; the fictional character played word games and puzzles with his granddaughter, Sophie Neveu, and created the codes and riddles that involved his own dead body in the novel's dramatic opening pages.

Robert Langdon

Professor Langdon was not invented for this novel; he appeared in Dan Brown's previous work, *Angels and Demons*, as the professor pitted against a secret society which was bent on destroying the Vatican with an anti-matter bomb. In order to save half of Rome from annihilation, Langdon had to decode old manuscripts, symbols and other clues in much the same way that he does in *The Da Vinci Code*.

His expertise in symbology, combined with Sophie Neveu's knowledge of codes and cyphers, is essential for *The Da Vinci Code* to have credibility: any other kind of hero could not realistically be expected to solve the endless brain-teasers that Langdon encounters on the Grail trail.

Bezu Fache

Dan Brown introduces another character with a direct association to the Rennes-le-Château area: Le Bézu is a tiny village just a couple of miles to the south of Bérenger Saunière's home.

It's so isolated that its church appears to be used for storing farm equipment.

From this village a dusty single track road leads higher into the mountain, becoming increasingly bumpy until it deteriorates into a mere footpath that leads to the peak where the scant ruins of Château des Templiers can be found.

This château of the Knights Templar forms the southernmost point of a perfect natural pentacle of hilltops upon which stand churches and ruined châteaux including Rennes-le-Château and the ruins of Blanchefort.

The pentacle is a symbol which the novel makes clear is representative of the power of the sacred feminine, as worshipped in the pre-Christian era, and as such is heretical to the Catholic Church.

Bezu Fache's surname means 'anger' in French, which certainly reflects his character in the novel.

Sophie Neveu

Sophie mentions that her grandfather, Jacques Saunière, used to joke that she was half divine because of the letters 'phi' in her name, which is a mathematical term for the divine proportion of 1.618:1. Her comment turns out to be ironic at the end of the novel when it is revealed that she is a direct descendant of Jesus through both sides of her parentage.

Her childhood nickname, Princess Sophie, provides a

convenient coincidence with the initials P.S. standing for Priory of Sion as well as hinting at her illustrious lineage.

Silas

Silas the albino belongs to the Catholic sect, Opus Dei, some members of which have been reported to practice corporal mortification using a barbed cilice belt around the thigh. Intended for mild use for just a couple of hours a day, the result is little more than discomfort or slight pain and has the effect both of dampening sexual desire and of experiencing in small, safe doses some of the suffering Jesus is believed to have endured on the cross.

In the novel, Silas takes corporal mortification to extremes that are unlikely to be encountered amongst the real Opus Dei membership.

Sir Leigh Teabing

Representing a typically exaggerated American view of Englishness that brings to mind Lee Evans' architect persona in the film *There's Something About Mary*, Leigh takes his first name from one of the authors of *The Holy Blood and the Holy Grail*, Richard Leigh, and his surname is an anagram made from the letters of the last name of the book's co-writer, Michael Baigent. It is a tribute that was not appreciated by those writers who subsequently issued a writ against Dan Brown's publisher for plagiarism of ideas, claiming that the 'whole jigsaw puzzle' of the novel is based on the years of research presented in their book.

By enlisting the help of a knight, *Sir Leigh Teabing*, in Langdon's Grail quest, Dan Brown is true to the ancient tradition of Grail legends.

Bishop Manuel Aringarosa

The president-general of Opus Dei in the novel has a surname in Italian that is almost a literal translation of 'red herring', although 'rosa' also hints at a connection to the rose symbol.

André Vernet

As well as sharing his surname with some famous French painters, this manager of the fictional Swiss bank vault also shares his name with a spa town just a few miles to the south of Rennes-le-Château, Vernet les Bains. Again, Dan Brown ties one of his characters to this region of southern France.

Rémy Legaludec

Leigh Teabing's manservant secretly works for the Teacher. His first name is taken from the Cognac brand Rémy Martin, and it is a poisoned Cognac drink that kills him in the novel.

Real people and organisations in the novel

Leonardo da Vinci

This multi-talented Renaissance artist and scientist was born in 1452, which for a man of such genius was perhaps centuries before his time. He invented ideas for powered flight, battle tanks and other modes of transport. He studied human anatomy by exhuming and dissecting bodies.

Leonardo may even have invented photography: some historians claim that the Turin Shroud is actually a photographic image on linen of Leonardo's own body.

Leonardo was a homosexual and a heretic. He resented the established Church but had no moral problem in earning money from it whenever it commissioned a painting from him. But he liked to put as much heretical imagery as possible into his Christian canvases.

Leonardo died in France in 1519. In the room where he spent his final moments were his two favourite paintings, *The Mona Lisa* and his last masterpiece, *St John the Baptist*.

Opus Dei

The sinister, shadowy sect portrayed in *The Da Vinci Code* is not quite the reality. Opus Dei is a personal prelature of the Catholic Church, which means it is a fully legitimate part of the mainstream religion. It is a 'personal' prelature because it is defined by individuals, whereas other Catholic subsets are defined by geographical areas, such as parishes. Opus Dei is not the kind of establishment suited for monks like Dan Brown's character Silas: its raison d'être is to help Catholics to find ways to serve God in their daily lives and in the community, rather than being locked away out of sight. But Opus Dei has gained a notoriety since revelations referred to by Dan Brown that it uses brainwashing and the 'dangerous' practice of corporal mortification. The self-harm implied in this latter description is not in reality as severe as Dan Brown shows it to be through Silas; and a certain amount of brainwashing occurs in all mainstream religions anyway, but because it is primarily done to children by parents, teachers and clergy it is somehow less controversial.

The Knights Templar

This legendary order of medieval knights was founded in the early twelfth century in order to protect pilgrims visiting the Holy Land, but quickly became involved in excavations beneath the Temple Mount in Jerusalem.

The Knights Templar are rumoured to have discovered something of major religious significance but no proof exists as to the precise nature of this find.

Speculation among historians has included the discovery of the Ark of the Covenant, a hoard of treasure, or evidence relating to the life of Jesus and Mary.

This last possibility would explain, according to the theory that is the basis of *The Da Vinci Code*, why the Templars became associated with the search for the Holy Grail. Could it be that they began a search for the bloodline of Jesus?

The reputation of the Knights Templar as a formidable fighting force led to the first banking system. Wealthy landowners would deposit their money with the knights and pay them to protect it. This proved so lucrative that the order became hugely wealthy, and finally attracted the jealous attention King Philip of France who arranged for all Knights Templar to be arrested throughout the land on the same day in order that he could have them executed on charges of heresy, then help himself to their banking system, properties and wealth.

Rennes-le-Château is in the centre of a circle of forts and castles belonging to the Knights Templar: Château des Templiers, Château de Blanchefort, plus Campagne sur Aude and about a dozen other fortresses all stand guard within a five mile radius of this hilltop village. What could there have been in Rennes-le-Château that could have justified this massive concentration of Templar resources?

President Mitterrand

The former French president had a strong interest in the mystery of Rennes-le-Château, making a high profile visit to the village in 1981. Not long after that date he masterminded the renovation works at the Louvre that culminated in the construction of the pyramids under one of which, according to *The Da Vinci Code*, lies the Holy Grail.

Was Dan Brown simply making use of a convenient connection between fiction and reality, or was Mitterrand really involved in the secrets of the Holy Grail?

The Priory of Sion

This 'secret society' popped up during Henry Lincoln's initial research into Rennes-le-Château. Supposedly an order set up in medieval times to protect the bloodline of Jesus, The Priory of Sion is now considered by many to be an elaborate twentieth-century forgery instigated by Pierre Plantard in 1967. He created documents, known as the *Dossiers Secrets*, to 'prove' his claim to the French throne and left them at the Bibliothèque National in Paris for researchers to find.

The following is a list of the Grand Masters of the Priory of Sion, according to Plantard's documents.

Grand Masters of the Priory of Sion

Jean de Gisors	1188-1220
Marie de Saint-Clair	1220-1266
Guillaume de Gisors	1266-1307
Edouard de Bar	1307-1336
Jeanne de Bar	1336-1351
Jean de Saint-Clair	1351-1366
Blanche d'Evreux	1366-1398
Nicholas Flamel	1398-1418
René d'Anjou	1418-1480
Iolande de Bar	1480-1483
Sandro de Filipepi	1483-1510
Leonardo da Vinci	1510-1519
Connétable de Bourbon	1519-1527
Ferdinand de Gonzague	1527-1575
Louis de Nevers	1575-1595
Robert Fludd	1595-1637
J. Valentin Andrea	1637-1654
Robert Boyle	1654-1691
Isaac Newton	1691-1727
Charles Radclyffe	1727-1746
Charles de Lorraine	1746-1780
Maximilian de Lorraine	1780-1801
Charles Nodier	1801-1844
Victor Hugo	1844-1885
Claude Debussy	1885-1918
Jean Cocteau	1918-1963

However, even if the Priory of Sion was a figment of Pierre Plantard's fertile imagination, it so happens that all the names on the list had connections with Freemasonary, alchemy, the Rosicrucian order or other secret organisations.

Robert Boyle and Isaac Newton were dedicated alchemists, the latter also reputedly a Rosicrucian as was Leonardo da Vinci.

So Plantard didn't just pluck random names out of thin air: some serious research went into choosing appropriate characters from history to populate his list.

The main locations in the novel

Ritz Hotel - Paris

The Paris Ritz is a more modest institution than its garishly-lit sister building in London. The Ritz name is only visible in a subtle script on the small white awnings on its front windows that face into the grand square that is Place Vendôme. The hotel is now famous for being the starting point of Princess Diana's final journey, and security is tight

– non customers are turned away at the revolving door. With room prices almost high enough to buy Sophie Neveu's Smart car within a week, Robert Langdon's sponsor, The American University of Paris, is clearly an educational institution that is not strapped for cash.

Musée du Louvre – Paris

Based on the site of a twelfth-century château, the remains of which still exist in the basement of the museum, the Louvre was remodelled by various French kings into a private building appropriate for a royal art collection, then, after the Revolution, into a public museum. The Grand Gallery that features so prominently in the opening chapters of *The Da Vinci Code* was one of two wings added to join the Louvre and Tuileries palaces, the latter of which burned down in 1871 and has since disappeared. This leaves the long arms of the Louvre extending westwards like a giant set of ornate tweezers by the bank of the Seine.

The Louvre was visited by Leonardo da Vinci.

Pyramid inversée

This inverted glass pyramid points dramatically down to a small solid marble pyramid beneath it, but the two are not, as Dan Brown claims, perfectly aligned. There is actually a noticeable misalignment of several inches between the glass pyramid's point and the marble peak. The mystical feeling experienced by Langdon in the novel is hard for the typical visitor to this pyramid to share not only because the spot marks the entrance to a bustling underground shopping centre, but also because the small, solid pyramid emerging from the floor is usually obscured by bored school-trip children sliding down the smooth sloping surfaces.

St Sulpice – Paris

Almost identical in its floor plan and outward appearance to its close neighbour, Notre Dame cathedral, St

Sulpice is a working place of worship that has innocently found itself at the heart of Dan Brown's novel and is hence inundated with tourists on the Da Vinci trail. Built on the site of a smaller church but at a slightly different angle, St Sulpice contains an unusual astronomical gnomon in the form of a huge white obelisk linked to a bronze meridian line laid into the floor. The line cuts across the centre of the church at a rather awkward angle, ending at a marble plaque. This line is mistakenly referred to as the old French meridian line, which does cut through Paris but which doesn't intersect St Sulpice.

It is likely that Dan Brown chose St Sulpice as a location in his novel partly for the presence of the rose line and partly because it is the cathedral to which Bérenger Saunière went seeking help with the translation of his coded parchments.

Bois de Boulogne - Paris

A strip of parkland between Boulevard Périphérique and the Seine on the western edge of Paris, the Bois de Boulogne is home to a large campsite, sports tracks and a few hundred prostitutes, but it is distinctly lacking in Swiss bank vaults and a Rue Haxo. In fact, Rue Haxo does exist, but it can be found not in the Bois de Boulogne area but on the other side of the city. Even then, it turns out, the bank is a fictional addition to the otherwise factual locations in the novel.

Temple Church - London

Robert Langdon thinks this London church is a vital link in the trail of clues leading to the Grail, but it actually proves to be a misinterpretation on his part. The distinctly round-shaped part of the church was built in 1185 in honour of the Virgin Mary by the Knights Templar order in the style of the circular Church of the Holy Sepulchre in Jerusalem, and became the headquarters of the

Templars in Britain. The church is famous for the carved effigies of Templar knights that lie dotted around its floor.

Westminster Abbey - London

Better known for its royal weddings and coronations than for its Grail connections, this twelfth-century cathedral faces the Houses of Parliament in central London. With a memorial to Isaac Newton, the alchemist and Rosicrucian who also makes it onto the list of Grand Masters of the Priory of Sion, it was essential that Dan Brown have his characters stop here before pushing on to Rosslyn. The Chapter House where Robert Langdon and

Sophie Neveu are cornered by an armed
Leigh Teabing was used for meetings of
the British Parliament in the fourteenth
century.

Rosslyn Chapel - Edinburgh

This extraordinary buttressed church
was built in Scotland by Sir William St
Clair in the fifteenth century and now
contains many generations of the St Clair
family in its crypts. Saint-Clair is the
name of Sophie Neveu's family in *The
Da Vinci Code*, and is a name that has
been connected with the descendants
of the Merovingian line and Jesus. Many
Grail-seekers visit this church in order
to study its dauntingly elaborate stone

carvings that cover just about every visible surface. The symbols of the Templars, Rosicrucians and Freemasons are all represented here, but whether those carvings hold the secret of the location of the Holy Grail remains a mystery.

Where is the real Rose Line?

Since 1884 the Prime Meridian line, an imaginary line running north to south across the planet, has run through Greenwich, England. But between 1667 and 1884 it ran through the centre of France, through Paris and further south through Rennes-les-Bains, a small spa town within walking distance of Rennes-le-Château. There is a small monument just outside the town to mark that fact.

Also known as the Rose Line, this zero-degrees meridian did not run through the cathedral of St Sulpice as claimed in *The Da Vinci Code*, but passed through Paris a few hundred yards to the side of that location. Rosslyn Chapel in Scotland takes its name from Rose Line, but no actual 'line' runs through it (not even the former Prime Meridian).

In Scottish Gaelic 'Rose Line' means 'brood of twelve', which implies that this is a site more related to a line of ancestry than geography. Is the line of the rose the same as the line of descendants of Jesus and Mary?

The key to the themes in the novel

Symbology

Robert Langdon's professional discipline is 'Religious Symbology', which is not a term used at Harvard for any of its academic subjects. Symbols are mentioned throughout *The Da Vinci Code* especially in connection with religious architecture and paintings, the most significant of which are discussed in the following pages.

Pagan Symbolism in Chartres Cathedral

The subject of the lecture that Robert Langdon is said to have given the evening prior to the events in the novel taking place is that of pagan symbolism in the architecture of the twelfth-century cathedral at Chartres. This building, which is dedicated to the Virgin Mary, has its internal and external walls and windows crammed with symbolic carvings and images.

A giant thirteenth-century rose window above the western entrance symbolises the sacred feminine, a bold and blatant pagan sign which shows the masons were cocking a snoop at their Christian employers. As if this didn't lay on the message thickly enough, the floor of the cathedral is dominated by an enormous labyrinth pattern showing tightly folded curves around a central flower, and this again was a pagan symbol of the vagina and hence of the sacred feminine. Whoever managed to con the bishop into granting permission to build it under the pretext that it could have a Christian interpretation must have been laughing their hessian socks off.

As well as paganism in the structure there are some other curiosities worthy of note. A carving above the north door officially depicts a coronation of Mary –

supposedly the Virgin Mary, but she looks to be the same age as Jesus so it could easily be Mary Magdalene – seemingly showing her to have equal divinity with Jesus. Could it instead represent the marriage of Jesus and Mary?

The Mary Magdalene stained-glass window depicts her arriving by boat in the south of France. This is actually the cathedral's own description of the window, although it fails to comment on the panes just below that show people having sex.

In this one window there is a fusion of paganism – the worshipping of the female form through lovemaking – and heretical Christianity showing Mary coming to France. But this isn't the only reference to Mary in France to be found within the Catholic Church: St Maximim in Provence claims to have Mary's skull on display as a relic. Tombstones depicting Mary on the cross, not Jesus, can be found in many French graveyards. The cult of Mary represents, in fact, a substantial undercurrent of religious devotion in France. If she really went there, surely she could have done so with a child of Jesus, if not with Jesus himself? Did she flee to escape the same fate as John the Baptist, who some researchers believe may have been a close relative of hers?

The Pentacle

Now more commonly referred to as the 'pentagram', this five-pointed star symbolises, according to Dan Brown, the sacred feminine and the order and beauty of nature.

It was a pagan religious symbol for thousands of years before the orthodox Church hijacked it as a symbol of the five blooded points of Jesus on the cross and twisted the pagan usage of it into a sign of devil worship.

Using the 1:25,000 scale map of the area around Quillan, France, which includes Rennes-le-Château, it is possible to draw a perfect pentacle that passes through five natural rock peaks which include the ruined châteaux of Blanchefort and the Templars. The discovery by Henry Lincoln of this giant star symbol occurring with an accuracy that can be measured to just a few feet is all the more amazing when you realise that the builders of the monuments and châteaux on the five points could not have measured the positions correctly without the benefit of aerial mapping, for the terrain is steep and rugged throughout the area. Did they benefit from a technology for measuring distances over mountainous land 'as the crow flies' that has since been lost to history?

Phi

Phi is a mathematical term for the 'divine proportion', or 1.618:1 (not to be confused with Pi which is 3.14). It is a ratio that frequently occurs in nature and which produces aesthetically pleasing proportions. It can be seen in insect bodies, leaves and plants, and Leonardo da Vinci demonstrates the presence of Phi in the human body in his drawing of the *Vitruvian Man* (as depicted on the cover of this book).

The measurement of a human from head to toe divided by the distance from belly button to toe will always equal Phi. The distance across a perfect pentacle will always be 1.618

**times the combined length of
two of its sides.**

The divine proportion was commonly
used by Renaissance architects to create
buildings and rooms in which the length
would be 1.618 times the width, which
always gave pleasing results.

Painters, too, used those proportions
in creating visually satisfying works of art.
Nicolas Poussin is said to have employed
the principles of Phi and pentacle in his
painting *Les Bergers d'Arcadie* (also
depicted on the cover of this book).

Symbolism in paintings

The Mona Lisa

Painted by Leonardo da Vinci at the beginning of the sixteenth century, this portrait has become the most famous work of art in the world thanks to the hype of nineteenth-century art critics who raved about the sitter's enigmatic smile. The painting's profile was further raised following a notorious theft in 1911 and an act of vandalism in 1956. Now located near the far end of the Grand Gallery in the Louvre behind tinted, bullet-proof glass, Leonardo's most celebrated masterpiece is almost permanently obscured by eager crowds taking photos that won't come out due to the reflection of the flash on the glass.

Recently theorists have proposed that the bizarre half smile of the subject may be hiding more than meets the eye: they have likened the woman's features to those of the artist himself, and have suggested that maybe the painting is actually a self portrait of Leonardo in drag.

This would seem to fit the character of the genius behind the brush who enjoyed practical jokes and incorporating symbols and dual meanings into his art.

The Madonna on the Rocks

Leonardo da Vinci's painting is actually called the *Virgin on the Rocks*: the title was changed to *Madonna on the Rocks* by Dan Brown in order to be able to provide suitable letters for the anagram 'so dark the con of man'. It contains what seems to be a giant rock penis behind the head of the Virgin Mary, which is about as pagan a symbol as you could ever encounter.

The Last Supper

Another masterpiece by Leonardo, there are several hints in this fresco that Mary Magdalene has a greater significance than the Church would accept. The figure to Jesus' right hand side, leaning away from him, is clearly that of a woman, even though all of the disciples were supposed to be men.

Is this a sign that Jesus and Mary were in a close relationship, possibly even married?

There is also a distinct void between them in the shape of a 'v', which is a symbol of the divine feminine for it represents the shape of the womb. At the base of the 'v' is where the Holy Grail should be if it were a mere cup, but nothing is there.

Is Leonardo hinting that Mary's womb is, instead, the Holy Grail? When looking at the combined body shapes of Jesus and Mary the letter 'm' can be seen: again, is this hinting that we should be paying more attention to Mary than to Jesus? This possibility is central to the theme of *The Da Vinci Code*.

Les Bergers d'Arcadie

Painted by Nicolas Poussin in the first half of the seventeenth century, the painting depicts shepherds trying to read the inscription on an old tomb they have discovered, which enigmatically spells out 'ET IN ARCADIA EGO' (literally: And in Arcadia I). The landscape in the background still matches the view from the site of a former tomb near the village of Arques and shows clearly Mount Cardou, the Blanchefort outcrop and Rennes-le-Château.

Between discovering coded parchments and becoming immensely wealthy, Bérenger Saunière purchased a copy of this painting during his first visit to Paris. The geometric and textual clues are believed by some investigators to have been crucial in Saunière's cracking of the parchment codes. *Les Bergers d'Arcadie* is not specifically mentioned in *The Da Vinci Code* (although Sir Leigh Teabing has an unnamed Poussin hanging in his home), but one of the two versions of this painting hangs in the Richelieu wing of the Louvre.

The reliability of history

Dan Brown makes the interesting point that history books are written by the winners. The point of view of the losers is never heard. Almost two thousand years of European history have been dominated by the point of view of Christians, for they were the clear winners in the battle for religious and philosophical influence. Therefore Dan Brown maintains a healthy distrust of the accepted view of history, and by opening his mind to other possibilities finds that there are hints and signs everywhere that perhaps all is not as it seems.

We will never know for sure what really happened in Judea two millennia ago. The human memory is a notoriously unreliable tool: most people struggle to recall details in their lives from the previous few weeks, let alone years.

The accounts of the life of Jesus were written long after his death, so it is possible that an element of fiction, distortion or misunderstanding might have crept into the details. Combine this dilution of the facts with the subsequent editing of the texts to suit the needs of the Church and what remains could be descibed as little more than propaganda.

One thing is certain according to *The Da Vinci Code*: the closest we are likely to come to the truth about that era is not the text of the New Testament. The Bible cannot be taken as gospel. It is in the coded and hidden messages of those who tried to preserve an unedited version of history for future generations that the truth may be found.

The search for the Holy Grail and its meaning

The Da Vinci Code is a modern interpretation of an age-old theme, the quest for the Holy Grail. Traditionally the Grail has been thought of as a cup from which Jesus drank at the Last Supper, an item curiously missing from Leonardo da Vinci's famous painting and one often associated with the legend of King Arthur. Its very existence as a cup is highly doubtful given that the first literary mention of it occurred in a fictional work by Chrétien de Troyes in the twelfth century. This hasn't prevented various institutions from claiming to be in possession of this elusive relic, however, most notably at Valencia cathedral in Spain.

So if the Grail is not a cup, then is it really what Dan Brown claims it to be in the novel: the bloodline of Jesus and Mary? How could such a big secret be kept for two thousand years without being lost forever?

Right under the parson's nose

It is possible that the early Catholic Church suppressed knowledge of aspects of the beginnings of Christianity that didn't fit its 'branding', and aggressively stamped out attempts at public discussion by burning as witches or heretics anyone holding contrary opinions. If this were indeed the case then it is entirely understandable that aggrieved parties would wish to preserve their understanding of the 'truth' in some way that would last for many centuries but which would not attract unwelcome attention from the Church.

The crucial knowledge to be passed on to future generations may have included:

- **the presence of Mary – and possibly Jesus – in France**
- **the family tree that dates back to the union of Mary and Jesus**
- **the true status of Mary as a senior disciple or fellow prophet**
- **the pagan ideas and symbols that were twisted, converted or hidden by the Church.**

The most durable substance available for the preservation of this knowledge was stone, but the only substantial buildings being made of stone in this period were those commissioned by the Catholic Church: the cathedrals. Hence the secret society of Freemasons evolved in order to encode heretical learning right under the very noses of the clergy from whom they were hiding it.

Again, it is one of those concepts that makes new sense of some disparate aspects of history. You couldn't build a cathedral without skilled stonemasons. You couldn't get work as a stonemason without belonging to the guild of Freemasons. The Freemasons created a secret society whose aim was the preservation of the knowledge suppressed at that time by the Church, and they were smart enough to encode that knowledge into the proportions, shapes and detailed carvings of the cathedrals they built for their unsuspecting employers.

Take, for example, a typical church door. It is shaped in an arch with a circular decorative window above. The window could be enormous, as it is in Chartres Cathedral, or smaller as in many town churches. This combination of arch and circle or flower is symbolic of the sacred feminine, a concept central to pre-Christian spiritual belief in which the woman was worshipped as the vessel from which came forth new life.

It may even have been a part of the early Christian church before its fourth century rebranding degraded the importance and role of women by edging Mary Magdalene from her place at the side of Jesus to the sidelines where she is scarcely mentioned.

The arched door represents the vagina and the flowery window represents the clitoris. Thus right at the entrance of a holy Christian temple the masons have ensured that the congregation passes through a massive symbol of pagan religion.

Heretical knowledge was also preserved over the centuries by learned individuals such as Leonardo da Vinci and other secretive societies such as the Rosicrucians. All used methods such as art, architecture, symbolism or just plain secrecy to pass on information to future generations whilst all the time living in fear of discovery by a viciously unforgiving Catholic Church. Why would they risk their lives, having seen the hideous tortures and executions of those who were caught, in order to preserve this knowledge? It must have involved something sufficiently earth-shattering to warrant that kind of chance.

The whole idea of secret societies and hidden knowledge is dismissed by some cynics as conspiracy theorist claptrap.

But history has shown time and again that when a repressive régime takes control of a population secret organisations very quickly develop in order to preserve beliefs, practices and learning.

When France was occupied by Nazis in the Second World War, for instance, the underground Résistance movement evolved, along with secret codes and symbols in order for them to be able to communicate without the dominant Germans knowing. A sudden and unforgiving expansion of Christianity across Europe would have driven people and their ideas underground in the same way.

Rennes-le-Château

If the key to *The Da Vinci Code* lies anywhere, it is to be found in a small village sitting atop one of the foothills of the Pyranees in south-west France. Exposed to harsh winds but blessed with views of breathtaking expanse, Rennes-le-Château is the only village you're ever likely to see where the welcome sign also forbids any digging of tunnels or excavation.

Formerly known as Rhedae, it was once the capital of its region with picture-postcard medieval castle defences all around in a similar style to the fairytale-style fortified city of Carcassonne, some twenty miles to the north. But Rennes-le-Château was destroyed in the late twelfth century by the King of Aragon, and what little remained became unoccupied ruins following the plague that hit soon after.

It would take five hundred years for this dormant settlement to come back to life. In the eighteenth century, the stones from the ruined fortifications were used to build a small number of

houses and the village of Rennes-le-
Château was born. An isolated, poor
farming community separated from the
nearest road by a steep thirty-minute
walk, the folk of this village led simple,
unpretentious lives, watched over by
their priest who lived in a dilapidated
presbytery next to their crumbling
church.

But the villagers had beneath them a
secret that in 1891 was to make their
priest a very wealthy man. As will be
shown, this secret is the key to *The Da
Vinci Code*.

The Saunière story

Bérenger Saunière was appointed priest of Rennes-le-Château in 1885. He found his little church almost in ruins, with a leaking roof that made it unfit for accommodating the spiritual needs of the population of two hundred.

His own presbytery was completely uninhabitable, forcing him to rent lodging in a nearby house. Saunière was always a determined and energetic character, however, and instantly set about trying to raise funds to repair the church. A small bequest of six hundred francs from one of his predecessors kick-started the most urgent repairs, following which Saunière was able to secure a loan of fourteen hundred francs (despite having no idea of how he could repay it) from the local government to tackle the second wave of restoration.

These works involved removing a Visigothic pillar that supported the altar, and inside this pillar he is reported to have found some ancient parchments. Initially at a loss to understand the coded writings, he took them to Paris where he enlisted the translation help of Abbé Bieil of St Sulpice (a cathedral that features strongly in *The Da Vinci Code*).

Saunière returned to his village a wealthy man. He upgraded his plans for the renovation of the church from basic repairs to the creation of a lavish and unusual interior, aspects of which were inspired by St Sulpice cathedral. He designed strange visual and textual riddles and clues and incorporated them into the building in the form of statues, carvings, paintings, and designs on the ceiling and floor. He also restored his presbytery and then built a luxurious house, the Villa Bethania, in front of it, in which he would entertain his new-found sophisticated Parisian friends. He bought the land to the north and east of the church and created formal gardens, ponds, a fountain, a miniature château-style library, a double-decker viewing gallery at the edge of the hill with a conservatory and an orangery.

Not all of his money was spent on himself: on behalf of all the villagers he funded the construction of a water tower to supply all the households with running water, making redundant the elegant cast iron circular hand pump which had previously been shared by all. He also upgraded the muddy track leading to the village to a proper road. After several clashes with his bishop and with the Vatican over his extraordinary lifestyle, Saunière died in 1917 amid rumours of poisoning.

Despite repeated pressure from many people to reveal the source of his wealth, Saunière told only two people: Marie Denarnaud, his housekeeper, who took the secret to her grave, and his close friend Abbé Rivière, who was reported to look deathly pale after their meeting and never laughed again in his life. What kind of secret could have had such a strong impact on his friend?

Many people have assumed that Saunière found some kind of buried treasure, to which the mysterious parchments led him, and it is true that the Rennes-le-Château region is potentially awash with stashes of ancient riches. Much of the surrounding land, particularly near Rennes-les-Bains, is now heavily wooded whereas in Saunière's day there would have been more bare rock due to constant tree felling for firewood. So if Saunière found a cave containing treasure its entrance would be much harder to spot today.

But is the idea of hidden treasure sufficient to explain the devastating effect Saunière's secret appeared to have on Abbé Rivière?

Did the ancient parchments reveal something far more fundamental about the origins of Christianity, the relationship between Jesus and Mary, the locations of their bodies or the existence of their descendants?

The theories about Saunière and their relationship to *The Da Vinci Code*

1. Did Saunière find the treasure of the Knights Templar?

When the Knights Templar were rounded up and executed in 1307 their treasure – said to be the fabulous lost treasure of Jerusalem – was not recovered. Was it hidden near Rennes-le-Château, at the Templar castle at Le

Bézu where they made their final stand before their eradication in the fourteenth century?

It's a plausible theory. The parchments may indeed have led Saunière to this treasure, and if so then this can't substantiate the main theme of the novel. But if the whole purpose of the Knights Templar was to seek and protect the Holy Grail, as some experts claim, then by logical progression their role is to protect the descendants of Jesus.

This is precisely what Jacques Saunière had tried to do in *The Da Vinci Code*.

2. Did Saunière find the treasure of the Merovingian kings?

The tombs of Merovingian kings that are rumoured to lie in sealed crypts beneath Rennes-le-Chateau could still contain fabulous amounts of gold (depending on whether or not they were plundered).

The Merovingians certainly had a presence in Rhedae: workers building the road to the village – a project funded by Saunière – in 1908 found hundreds of skeletons of Merovingian origin, possibly buried following a battle on the slopes of the hill.

It was traditional for Merovingian kings to be buried with their most valuable possessions. Saunière's housekeeper Marie once remarked that the villagers were walking on gold without realising it. Could it have been Merovingian gold?

The Merovingian dynasty ended in 751, though it was the murder of Dagobert II in 679 that is seen as the mortal blow from which the line could not recover. It brought to an end a line of kings reputed to be descended from the union of Mary Magdalene and Jesus. But they were not extinct: Dagobert had a son, Sigisbert, who supposedly continued to flow the holy DNA down through history.

In *The Da Vinci Code*, Sophie Neveu's

lineage could be traced directly to the
Merovingian kings and to Jesus and Mary.
Bérenger Saunière's discovery of the
tombs of such kings could be the source
of his riches, though it would not verify
the claim that these royals were related
to Jesus and Mary since no documentary
proof exists of this connection.

3. Did Saunière find gold nuggets in a river?

The small and almost ruined château at
Rennes-le-Château could have been a
location where alchemy was attempted
– one of its tall towers is rumoured by
some commentators to have been built
for the purpose of alchemical practices.

Whether or not this was really the case, it's entirely possible that substantial quantities of gold could have existed in the château at the time of the French Revolution: in addition to all the famous treasures lost in the region over the centuries there are also gold mines in the local hills that were dug by the Romans.

In order to avoid the theft of the gold by revolutionaries, it has been suggested that gold nuggets were baked in clay to look like pebbles and deposited in a nearby stream – the plan being for the owner to retrieve them in calmer political times but for whatever reason did not return to do so. This would explain Saunière's bizarre habit of collecting large pebbles in a basket in the valley below the village and walking back up to the church where he used them to build a grotto. Did he secretly smash them open looking for gold and disguise his actions by using the genuine stones for the grotto?

The tiny de Couleurs river runs to the south of Rennes-le-Château. It's only accessible on foot through fields and thick undergrowth until you come to a bubbling stream littered with hundreds of pebbles of the size Saunière used to collect. If some of them are fake stones containing gold then there's every chance that more of them still lie under the shallow water where they have remained undisturbed for hundreds of years.

Should this turn out to be the source of the priest's wealth then it would seriously undermine the validity of Dan Brown's argument, but this is hardly the kind of secret that would have the shock value of whatever it was Saunière told to his two confidantes.

4. Was there substantial heretical evidence in the parchments Saunière found?

If the parchments Saunière found inside the damaged altar contained or led to evidence of the bloodline of Jesus, and

the Vatican paid him vast amounts of
money not to tell anyone, this would be
the most direct vindication of the idea
behind *The Da Vinci Code*.

**Documents detailing the
marriage or sexual relationship
between Jesus and Mary
Magdalene would have been
highly damaging to the
nineteenth-century Catholic
Church, especially if there was
also evidence that Jesus had
survived the crucifixion and fled
to France with Mary (which
would explain why he was
spotted alive three days after
his alleged death).**

It's conceivable that the Vatican
would have bought Saunière's silence at

first, and then may have decided that he had become too extravagant and presented such a security risk that an easier solution would be to poison him. This would have had to involve his housekeeper, which might be why she was reported to have ordered his coffin ten days before his death in 1917 – even though he appeared fit and well at the time.

Dan Brown based his novel on the theory that Jesus and Mary produced a child, either in Jerusalem or in France. There is no incontrovertible evidence that this actually happened, only clues, symbols and literary and artistic hints that arguably point towards this hypothesis. If Saunière really found such proof, he broke it down into even more clues and riddles, thus ensuring that the secret would never be known during his lifetime. Similarly, in *The Da Vinci Code*, the same secret is protected for posterity by underground societies and codes that have evaded discovery for centuries.

5. Did the money come from Saunière's lover, Emma Calvé?

Saunière's illicit relationship with the celebrated Parisian singer Emma Calvé may have been so intense that she paid for all of the building works to his church, home and gardens in order that her time with him should be more luxurious. As a result of this, Saunière may simply have invented all of the strange clues that he left behind in order to throw people off the scent.

This is admittedly an unlikely scenario, but one which has some sympathy among local residents and which if true would prove highly embarrassing to all of the treasure hunters, conspiracy theorists and Dan Brown. But how could a humble priest get to mix in the elevated social circles necessary for an introduction to a singing star? Surely he could only find his way into that kind of company once he had money to spend?

6. Did Saunière find evidence that Jesus was buried within the pentacle of hills?

Rennes-le-Château forms one of the five outer points of a statistically unlikely but nevertheless genuine geometric pentacle of hilltop churches, castles and natural peaks. The pentacle was a pre-Christian symbol of the power of nature and birth, and it is possible that when Jesus died he was buried at the centre of this naturally occurring pattern in order that he might benefit from the pentacle's powers to bring him back to life. This would represent a fusion of pagan and Christian ideas that the Vatican would not want made public, so it may have paid Saunière to remain silent about his discovery.

For Jesus to be buried in France at all implies that he died there, and therefore would have had the opportunity to father a child. If this theory could be proven it would seriously strengthen the validity of *The Da Vinci Code*'s theme.

7. Was Saunière paid by Merovingian descendants for proof of their claim to the throne of France?

Saunière was known to have had communications with Archduke von Habsburg, who may have paid him for providing documents (or for at least having a good look for them in the church) relating to his family history. Whether this was for the Archduke's own curiosity or because he wanted to launch a serious attempt to reinstate the French monarchy with himself as king is unclear, but Habsburg was very likely a Merovingian descendant and by implication a relation of Jesus.

This theory would not prove Dan Brown's claims, but does not contradict them either.

The mysterious military mayor

All French towns and villages have a *Mairie* or town hall and a mayor. Normally the mayor of a small village such as Rennes-le-Château would be a local farmer or resident who would do the mayoral job on a part-time basis.

Recently Jean-François Lhuilier was appointed the new mayor of Rennes-le-Château. He is a retired Colonel from the French army paratroops regiment, sent down to the new posting from Paris.

This would seem a rather heavy-handedly militaristic decision to make for a population of two hundred people.

Is there something in the village of Rennes-le-Château that the French government wants to protect? Is Lhuilier responsible for keeping an eye on things and reporting back to the government?

The part of Saunière's formal gardens that is now a car park has also been used for military investiture ceremonies for new army recruits. Again, this is a strange choice of location considering there isn't even enough space in the village to park all the cars and trucks needed for such an occasion.

The Channel 4 documentary with Tony Robinson

In February 2005 Channel 4 first screened in the UK a documentary entitled *The Real Da Vinci Code*, presented by the *Time Team* host and *Blackadder* star Tony Robinson (who is also credited with editing the documentary, a highly unusual thing for a presenter to do – could it be that he cared so much about slanting the programme in a particular direction that he insisted on maintaining editorial control over the content?).

The programme attempted to disprove the theories in *The Da Vinci Code*, but its less-than-objective approach resulted in flawed journalism, some aspects of which are discussed on the following pages.

1. The search for the Grail in the documentary.

The documentary wasted the first half an hour talking about the Grail as a cup, which surely hardly anyone believes to be the case any more? A vessel yes, a human vessel for carrying a genetic bloodline through history, but not a cup. The time spent on this wild goose chase meant that crucial aspects of the Holy Grail subject were glossed over, especially Rennes-le-Château.

2. The lack of attention paid to Rennes-le-Château.

The biggest flaw in the Tony Robinson documentary was the dismissal of the mystery surrounding the source of Bérenger Saunière's wealth. The documentary claimed the money came from the sale of masses and showed Saunière's handwritten accounts to 'prove' it. Clearly Saunière was spending enormous sums of money way beyond the normal means of a poorly paid village priest in a tiny hilltop village. The renovated church, the water tower, the luxurious Villa Bethania, the folly-style library and ornate gardens that were all paid for from his own pocket could not escape the concerned attention of the new Bishop of Carcassonne, Monseigneur Beauséjour, in 1902. The bishop demanded accounts from Saunière showing the amount spent and the origin of the wealth. Saunière refused point blank to reveal the source of his money, but he did supply accounts showing that the renovation of his church and his other building work had cost 190,000 francs. In fact the true cost of the works was closer to a million francs, but Saunière needed to make it seem like he was less extravagant and wealthy than he really was.

At fifty centimes a mass, which was the going rate at the time, Saunière would have had to have sold two million masses to earn as much as he did.

Not only is that a physical impossibility for one man, but there wasn't even a big enough population in the area to create that level of demand.

Furthermore, Saunière's spending plans didn't stop at a million francs. When he died he had schemes already devised for further lavish construction projects, but instead the money was left to his housekeeper, Marie Denarnaud. When the French government replaced the currency after the Second World War in order to punish those who had profited by collaborating with the Germans (the old currency could only be exchanged if a person could prove how they had earned it), Marie was seen burying vast sums of cash in her garden at night rather than reveal the source of Saunière's wealth.

3. The significance of The Priory of Sion. Much of the documentary was given over to the claim that Pierre Plantard had faked the *Dossiers Secrets* that included the famous list of the Grand

Masters of the Priory of Sion. It's true to say that his self-aggrandising claims to be descended from the Merovingian king, Dagobert II, are now generally suspected to be lies. However, Plantard's self-created fantasy world was first constructed in 1956, nearly half a century after Saunière had died at Rennes-le-Château, so none of his forgeries change the fact that Saunière found something that made him wealthy.

The list of Grand Masters of the Priory of Sion provided by Plantard has always looked a little too impressive and convenient to be true. The early names are families that are possibly linked to the bloodline of Jesus, such as the Saint-

Clair (Sinclair) family which features in *The Da Vinci Code*. But later names like Isaac Newton, Victor Hugo and Claude Debussy seem to be there simply because they have connections with other secret societies which makes them look convincing in the Priory of Sion list. Why would the stewardship of such an important secret society switch from the families at its core to the famous artists and scientists of later years?

It seems more likely that two or more societies have been fused by Plantard: the original, medieval Priory of Sion or its equivalent, and then later members or Grand Masters of other orders such as the Rosicrucians.

4. *Missing the point at Rosslyn Chapel.*
Tony Robinson visited the chapel and declared there was nothing here but ten generations of the Sinclair family. Having dismissed the Sinclair tombs as irrelevant, he moved on. But that, surely, is the whole point of the search for the Grail according to *The Da Vinci Code*. The Grail *is* the descendants of Jesus, and that family tree includes the Merovingian line of kings from whom in turn are descended numerous groups including the Habsburg, Stuart and Devonshire families and, of course, the Sinclair family. So in fact Tony Robinson was standing over ten examples of the Holy Grail but he somehow missed the point.

Errors in
The Da Vinci Code
and their significance

Dan Brown states at the beginning of the novel that the Priory of Sion and Opus Dei are real organisations, and that the 'artwork, architecture, documents and secret rituals' described by him are 'accurate'. That page is headed by the simple word 'Fact'. This claim adds a chilling and intriguing layer of meaning to the story, as well as adding gravity to the novel's central concept about the existence of a bloodline of Jesus. But are the 'facts' really as Dan Brown portrays them?

Is it fair to assume that small errors in the book are examples of Brown's unreliability? There are many examples, including the utterly trivial typographic error where he omits the letter 'l' from the word 'looking' in the Epilogue (a surprising mistake to remain in a book after more than 25 print runs), the strange manner in which Paris' Gare St Lazare railway station in Chapter 33 becomes Gard du Nord in Chapter 35. Other geographic inventions include Rue

Haxo being in the Bois de Boulogne area and the incorrect route along which Langdon is driven from the Ritz hotel to the Louvre museum. The car he is in is said to go south past the Opera House through Place Vendôme, whereas in fact the journey must begin at Place Vendôme since that is that address of the Ritz, and the Opera House is located three blocks to the north in the opposite direction of the Louvre.

These are small details, but are they significant? If Brown can be wrong about this and other minor facts, could he be wrong about the major themes in the book? Or are we ignoring the incredibly complex job that one man faced alone in order to write this book and forgetting that fact is often twisted to create good fiction?

When people dismiss *The Da Vinci Code* on account of its small factual errors, are they simply trying to deflect attention from the larger themes which can neither be proved nor disproved?

In a way this is similar to the argument about whether or not it's correct to say that Jesus was married. It shouldn't matter if he were single or married. Surely the important thing is his message, his moral and philosophical teachings that can help us to make the world a better place. But what we see is clergymen spending more time arguing about whether to let women become bishops than practising the teachings of Christ.

Dan Brown has written a novel, not a Bible. He doesn't claim every word to be true, but the themes and concepts upon which the story is constructed deserve fair consideration.

Conclusion: the key

To speak of a da Vinci code sounds like *The Bible Code*, or some similar elaborate cypher system set up to hide secrets from everyone until such time as technology or intelligence has developed to a high enough degree to crack it. But Leonardo did not create a coherent code, per se. We know that he kept notes in a reverse handwriting which is easy to read with the use of a mirror, and that certain clues and heretical concepts were encoded into his paintings, but that isn't really what the key to *The Da Vinci Code* is about.

The novel begins with a search for a keystone which will lead to the Holy Grail and finishes with the revelation that the Holy Grail is in fact one of the story's main characters. Dozens of smaller codes and clues along the way are encountered but there is no single key to any of these, no 'rosetta stone' that will unlock a vast library of coded information.

When dealing with events that may or may not have happened two thousand years ago nothing can really be known for sure, especially if so many of the contemporary written accounts were banished by the portion of the Christian Church that became dominant. It is conceivable that the Vatican archives contain some or all of the missing material, preserved forever in the underground vaults that feature so strongly in Dan Brown's earlier novel, *Angels and Demons*, but unavailable for public scrutiny whilst the Catholic Church persists in its current form.

So if access to the Vatican secrets is impossible for all but those on the highest echelons of the Roman Catholic priesthood (none of whom would have any incentive to reveal them anyway) how can we ever find out if *The Da Vinci*

Code is correct? There is one other place which is as yet untapped but which could contain history-changing artefacts. A key to *The Da Vinci Code* does exist there. This key, when and if found, will either vindicate Dan Brown's ideas or will show his novel to be a story based on fiction, not fact.

The key is simple: it is the source of the mysterious wealth acquired by Bérenger Saunière in Rennes-le-Château in the late nineteenth century.

Many books have been written on the subject since *The Holy Blood and the Holy Grail* first brought to wide public attention the idea that perhaps the priest was paid by the Vatican or others not to disclose damaging religious secrets concerning a bloodline of Jesus. The currently available evidence is open to wide interpretation and can be used to support or deny the theory according to an author's religious predisposition or prejudice.

The more you investigate this subject, the more complex and convoluted it becomes. One piece of evidence leads you to several more pieces, each with their own multiple meanings, and there are many gaps in the trail which can be filled by any number of assumptions.

It's possible to dedicate an entire lifetime to the investigation of the vague and enigmatic clues and codes, as writers such as Henry Lincoln have famously done.

Very little of the evidence often cited is hard fact, even though many writers try to present it as such. Lincoln cleverly moved on from attempting to draw conclusions from the oddities to be found in this region of France and in his later books and interviews he allows others to find their own answers to the fascinating clues that he presents. He recognised that no matter what he wrote based on the evidence, there would always be another writer who would look at the same discovery and make a different interpretation.

Until extensive, authorised excavation takes place at Rennes-le-Château, the mystery of Saunière's money will never be solved and the legitimacy of the theory that he discovered evidence about the Holy Grail as a bloodline will never be known.

But if some real evidence exists beneath Rennes-le-Château, it would take a change in French law before it could be found. This is a village where digging has been illegal since 1965. Blocked off under the ticket office of the Saunière museum is the entrance to a tunnel that was begun in the early sixties and abandoned when the law came into force – just yards short of the church.

Many secret tunnels have been dug under private properties into the soft hilltop clay before and since that time, and the hilltop is probably a honeycomb of ancient and modern passages. Most of those tunnels were dug by treasure-hunters, since the local understanding through most of the last century was simply that Saunière had found gold. The church is a little too far from the nearest houses, however, for an amateur tunneler to reach and any crypts or vaults that it may possess remain sealed beneath its stone floor.

The church of St Peter, the original church of Rennes-le-Château when it was the powerful city of Rhedae, was destroyed along with the rest of the original buildings. But its location is different to that of the present day church, being on a higher ground level some yards to the north in a corner of Saunière's formal gardens where there is now a restaurant.

This is where excavations need to take place.

If the bodies of Jesus or Mary or their supposed descendants – the Merovingian kings – were buried in Rennes-le-Château then they are to be found in vaults deep beneath the site of St Peter's church.

The key to *The Da Vinci Code* is here, buried perhaps forever beneath the kitchens that prepare snacks and meals to thousands of tourists and treasure-hunters who visit the village each month.

Of course, if ancient bodies were to be found and carbon dated to the time of Christ, there is still no way of verifying their identities unless sufficient accompanying evidence was buried with them.

Even then it is likely that theories and counter-theories will continue the battle for intellectual supremacy for many years to come.

Bibliography

Andrews, Richard and Paul Schellenberger, *The Tomb of God*

Baigent, Michael; Richard Leigh and Henry Lincoln, *The Holy Blood and the Holy Grail*

Brown, Dan, *The Da Vinci Code*

Hopkins, Marilyn; Graham Simmans and Tim Wallacce-Murphy, *Rex Deus*

Lincoln, Henry, *Key to the Sacred Pattern*

Martin, Sean, *The Knights Templar*

Miller, Malcolm, *Chartres Cathedral*

Picknett, Lynn and Clive Prince, *The Templar Revelation*

Robinson, James (Ed), *The Nag Hammadi Library*

De Sède, Gérard, *The Accursed Treasure of Rennes-le-Château*

Useful websites

Dan Brown	www.danbrown.com
The Da Vinci Code	www.thedavincicode.com
The Knights Templar	www.templarhistory.com
Opus Dei	www.opusdei.org
The Louvre	www.louvre.fr
Rosslyn Chapel	www.rosslynchapel.org.uk
Temple Church	www.templechurch.com
Château de Villette	www.frenchvacation.com
Rennes-le-Château	www.renneslechateau.com
The Vatican	www.vatican.va
Nag Hammadi Library	www.gnosis.org/naghamm/nhl.html

Index

Appendix
Main locations visitor information

The Ritz Hotel, Place Vendôme, Paris
Open only for paying customers. www.ritzparis.com has details.

Musée du Louvre (and Pyramid inversée), Paris
Open every day except Tuesdays, from 9am to 6.45pm (9.45pm on Wednesdays and Fridays). Entry is free on the first Sunday of each month. Arrive early to avoid long queues. The Pyramid inversée is in the adjacent underground shopping centre so it's free to visit.

St Sulpice church, Place St Sulpice, Paris
Open daily, 7.30am to 7pm. Admission free. Look for the gnomon inside, and the adjacent sign: 'Contrary to fanciful allegations in a recent bestselling novel, this is not a vestige of pagan temple.'

Bois de Boulogne, Paris
Large green belt area to the west of Paris, alongside the Seine. Free to visit, but its main attractions are limited to trees and water.

Temple Church, (just off Fleet Street), London
Open Wednesday to Sunday, but visiting days and hours vary so check www.templechurch.com for details. Admission free.

Westminster Abbey, Parliament Square, London
Open Monday, Tuesday, Thursday, Friday 9.30am to 3.45pm; Wednesday to 7pm, Saturday to 1.45pm. Entry £8. Closed Sunday.

Rosslyn Chapel, Roslin, Midlothian, Scotland
Open Monday to Saturday, 10am to 5pm, and Sunday midday to 4.45pm. Admission £5 and worth every penny.